Angels and Demons

Coloring Book

Adult Colouring Books

Aryla Publishing 2019

978-1-912675-51-7

www.arylapublishing.com

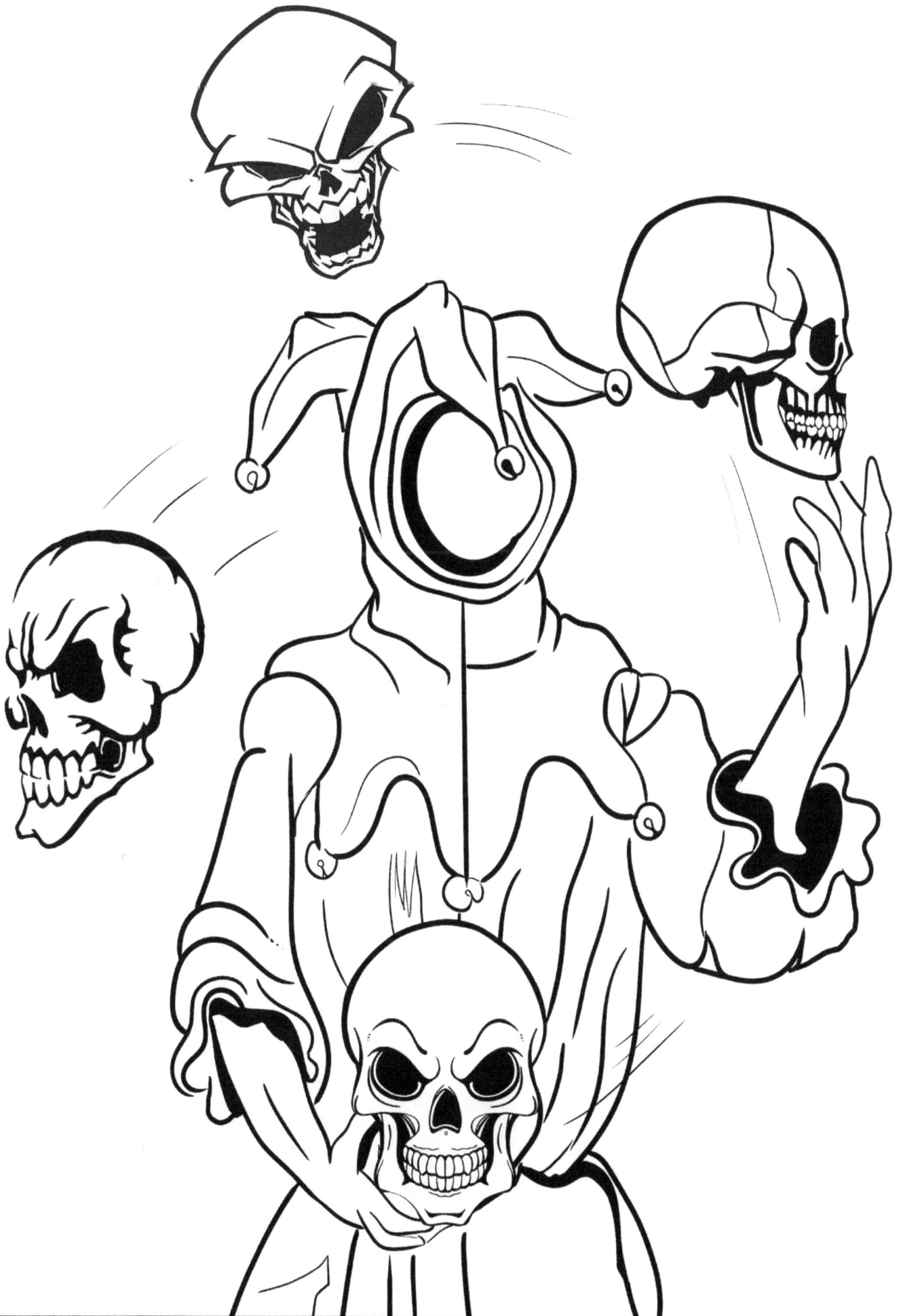

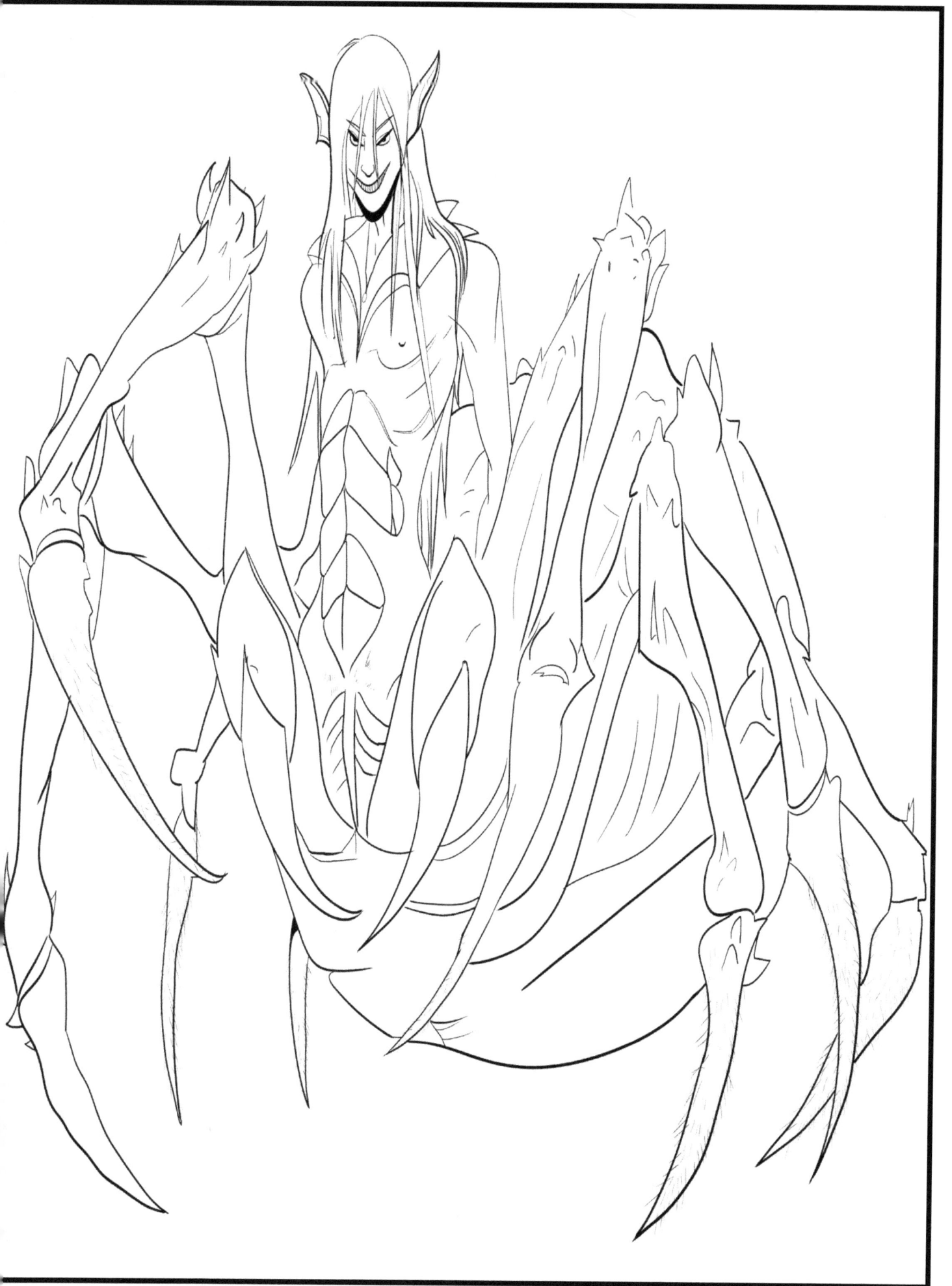

Thank you for purchasing this book.

If you would like to know more about Aryla Publishing Books please visit:-

www.ArylaPublishing.com

Or follow us on
Facebook
Twitter
Instagram
for *free promotions*

@arylapublishing

We would love to know what you think of this book so please leave us a review.

Have a wonderful day ☺

Other Coloring Books from Aryla Publishing

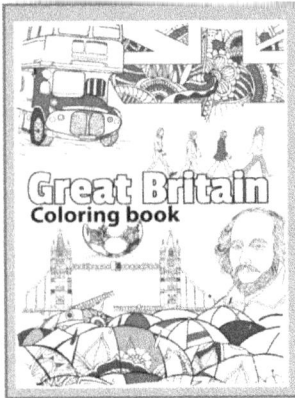

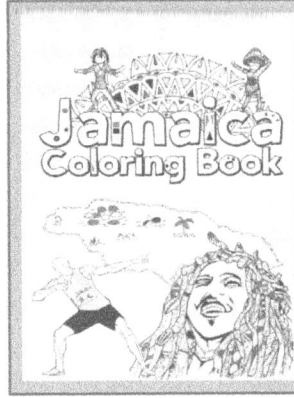

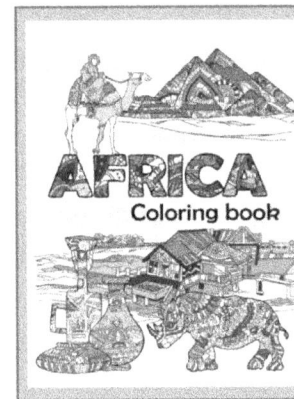

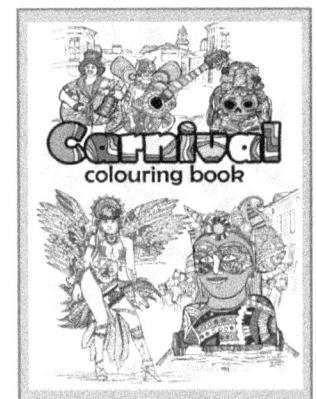

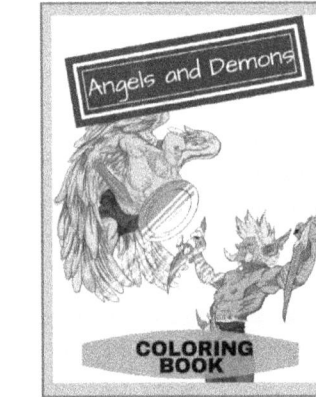

Great Britain Coloring book

U.S.A. Coloring book

Jamaica Coloring Book

Mexico Coloring book

PIRATE Coloring Book

DRAGON Coloring Book

UNICORN Coloring Book

MERMAIDS Coloring Book

Black Inventors Coloring Book

Black History Figures Coloring Book

AFRICA Coloring book

Carnival colouring book

1920'S COLORING BOOK

Kittens and Puppies COLORING BOOK

Black Brothers COLORING BOOK

Angels and Demons COLORING BOOK

JAPAN

FRANCE
Coloring Book

GREEK MYTHOLOGY

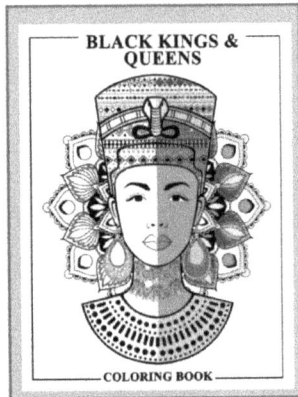
BLACK KINGS & QUEENS
COLORING BOOK

BLACK HEROES
Coloring Book

BLACK SISTERS

TAROT COLORING BOOK

CIRCUS
COLORING BOOK

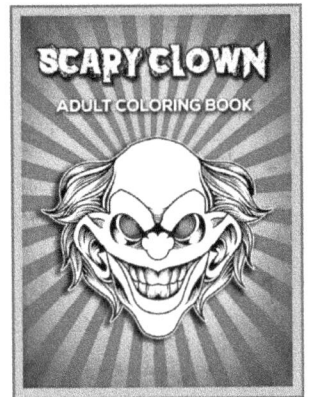
SCARY CLOWN
ADULT COLORING BOOK

ANIMAL COLORING BOOK

MYTHICAL CREATURES
Coloring Book

OWL
Coloring Book

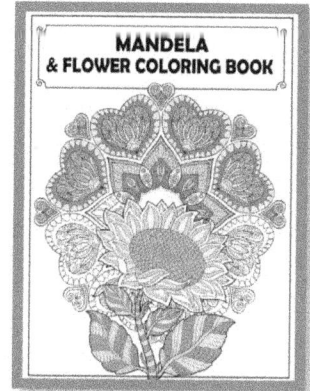

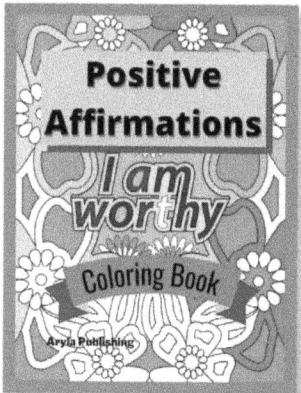

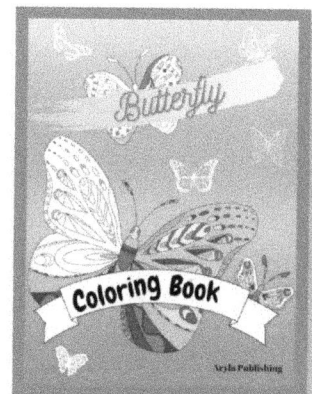

Visit **www.ArylaPublishing.com**

to find out about all new releases.

Follow us @arylapublishing on Twitter Instagram & Facebook

Search for Aryla Publishing on

▶ YouTube

Check out our <u>Book Trailers</u>

<u>Subscribe</u> **to keep up to date with new releases!**

WE WOULD LOVE
YOUR FEEDBACK

PLEASE LEAVE REVIEW AT:-

https://bit.ly/angelsdemonsreview

Or use the QR code below

www.ingramcontent.com/pod-product-compliance
Lightning Source LLC
Chambersburg PA
CBHW081723270326
41933CB00017B/3282